THE MIDDLE AGES

by Alan Clifford

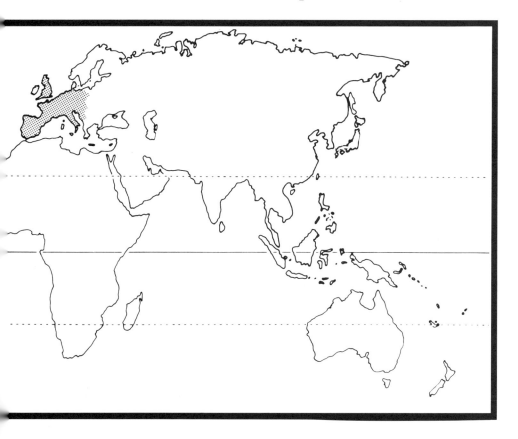

Greenhaven Press, Inc.
577 SHOREVIEW PARK ROAD
ST. PAUL, MN 55112

The castle of Canossa in northern Italy where Pope Gregory VII met and granted absolution to the Emperor Henry IV in 1076

THE MEETING AT CANOSSA

The meeting at Canossa in January 1077 marked a turning point in western European history. The Holy Roman Emperor Henry IV arrived at the fortress of Canossa in northern Italy to ask Pope Gregory VII to lift the sentence of *excommunication* (being cast out of the Church) which had been passed on him in 1076. It was one of the worst winters for many years. Pope Gregory's own account describes how Henry was forced to wait in the courtyard of the castle for three days before the Pope agreed to accept him back into the Church (D1)*. The sight of a king standing barefoot in the snow weeping as he asked for forgiveness would certainly have been extraordinary, although of course this is only the Pope's side of the story. But the real importance of the event was that it showed how bad relations between Pope and Emperor had become.

Throughout the previous two or three hundred years these two had generally regarded each other as friend and protector, and as partners in the just government of society. This partnership had its origins far back in history, in the days of the late classical Roman Empire, when a Pope said that the world was ruled by two powers — Pope and Emperor. The Pope needed the military support of the Emperor to protect himself and the Church's lands. The Emperor needed the Pope to make holy and binding the oath of loyalty of his subjects by crowning him, and also to give his rule the spiritual support it needed in an age when almost everyone believed in the power of God. The mutual

*The reference (D) indicates the numbered documents at the end of this book

The anointing of a king, from a French manuscript of the early fourteenth century showing a coronation ceremony

dependence of Pope and Emperor was sealed in A.D. 800 when the Pope crowned the Frankish king Charlemagne as 'Holy Roman Emperor'. The events surrounding the meeting at Canossa showed how weak this partnership had become.

THE FEUDAL SYSTEM

Medieval European rulers could not run their countries without soldiers. They paid their soldiers by granting them the money which could be earned from a piece of land. From this developed what we call the *feudal system*. The king (or emperor) gave *fiefs*

The ceremony of homage. Figures, representing the barons, bow before the Emperor in this late tenth century manuscript

The church is seen as an offering to God. In this mosaic king William II of Sicily (1166-89) offers the newly-built Monreale Cathedral to the Blessed Virgin

(revenues and taxes) and other privileges, usually from land, to his barons; in return they swore an oath to fight for him when he needed them. In turn the barons gave parts of their fiefs to knights; in return the knights swore to fight for the baron. Theoretically the feudal system could provide good government; in practice it led to frequent arguments about rights and duties and often to war. It was, though, at least a basis for government. But if the king were excommunicated the whole system fell apart because the barons were released from their oath to help him.

THE CHURCH

It is not possible to understand medieval Europe without realizing what an important part religion and the Church played in people's lives. When we look at the great size of the cathedrals and abbeys built then, we can begin to get some idea of the money and effort people were prepared to give to religion. In the dangers and uncertainties of life in the Middle Ages men and women felt they needed the protection of God, and wanted God's blessings during all the most important acts of their lives, especially birth, marriage and death. The Church was the agency through which they received God's blessing and they kept in touch with God through the Church services. The Church was also important because it organized law, education and many social services. To be excommunicated, that is to be cut off from the life of the Church,

was worse than being an outlaw because you were not only denied many of the benefits of society in this world but it was thought you had probably lost your chance in the next world too.

The medieval Church had a chain of authority, just as *lay* (non-Church) society had under the Emperor. At the top was the Bishop of Rome, or Pope, whose power was believed to descend from God, through Jesus and St Peter. The bishops drew spiritual power from the Pope and in turn passed it on to the parish priests who looked after the religious life of ordinary people.

CHURCH AND STATE

So there were two chains of power which ran side by side; a chain of spiritual power from Pope to priest and a chain of lay power from Emperor to knight. In theory they could exist happily side by side; in practice they did not, because at various points the two chains were tangled.

One point was at the bottom. Both Church and State relied on the wealth produced by the work of peasants on the land. How were they to share this wealth? Another way in which they were mixed up was through their claims to make and administer laws.

But the principal way was through government. The Pope was not only head of the Church; he was also a prince who ruled his own lands. By A.D. 1200 the Pope had more feudal *vassals* (men who had sworn to serve him) than anyone else. As a result the Pope had

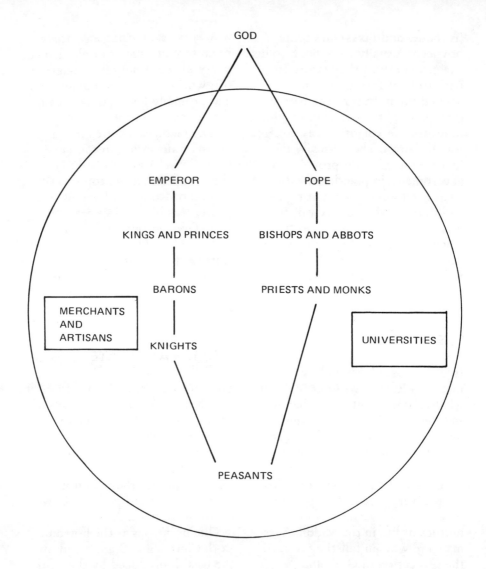

The two chains of power

not only spiritual power, but a great deal of lay power as well.

However, the main cause of the dispute between Henry IV and Gregory VII was that the Emperor needed the help of the bishops in order to govern.

THE CHURCH IN MEDIEVAL GOVERNMENT

Bishops and abbots (the heads of abbeys) often had so much power both in the Church and in government that kings and nobles had to have some control over them. For hundreds of years the Emperor was only able to run his kingdom by employing bishops as local officials. They collected taxes, made records of the law courts, and drew up lists of estates and farms. They also taught the basics of Christianity to the peoples who came newly under the rule of the Emperor.

No Emperor could do without the services of such men for no one else had any education. The Church was rewarded by the grant of large estates, but in return the Emperor insisted that he should have a say in the selection of bishops and abbots who also acted as civil servants. In such a system of government partnership between Pope and Emperor was essential.

MONASTERIES AND CHURCH REFORM

The clash between Church and State came about through a new, reforming movement in the Church. In the early Middle Ages

The Pope in council. He is being advised by his councillors both lay and clerical

A reconstruction of the interior of the Abbey of Cluny. It was the largest and most sumptuous church in western Christendom, and served as a model to many other Benedictine churches

the Church had been weak, and had been protected by kings and powerful nobles. In return, they had claimed a share of its wealth. Also, as the Church became more deeply involved in government, kings needed a say in how it should be run. For both reasons, the best jobs in the Church were going to friends and relatives of the king. The reformers wanted to put a stop to this and make sure that bishops and abbots were appointed by other churchmen (D2).

The reformers drew much strength from the monastery of Cluny in France. During the early Middle Ages monasteries had spread throughout Europe. In them men known as monks gave up worldly pleasures and devoted themselves to God. Many became centres of culture and played a valuable part in preserving and passing on the Latin classics. But many also became wealthy (D3) and the monks forgot their vows of poverty, chastity and obedience. An effort at reform and stricter discipline began at Cluny (founded in A.D. 910), where the monastery was organized so that there was no outside interference. Cluny and its daughter monasteries became training grounds for the reformers who wanted to extend the example of Cluny to all the Church. Gregory VII himself may have been a monk at Cluny before he became Pope.

THE CONTEST BETWEEN GREGORY VII AND HENRY IV

Pope Gregory wished to assert his supremacy over all kings, and the Emperor in particular (D4). In

Emperor Henry IV drawn by a German chronicler holding an orb and sceptre as symbols of his royal power

1075 a decree against lay appointment (*lay investiture*) was passed by a Church Council and led to the quarrel between Henry IV and Gregory. The dispute came to a head later in the year over the appointment of the Archbishop of Milan. The city of Milan controlled the prosperous lands of the Po valley in northern Italy. It was also an important staging post on the route south from Germany to Italy and Henry IV needed control of it to safeguard his north Italian estates. When Henry attempted to get one of his supporters appointed the Pope threatened to excommunicate him, and did so in 1076. This action not only cut the Emperor off from the life of the Church, but also, because his subjects were freed from their oath of loyalty to him, in effect took away his royal authority (D5).

Henry was already having difficulty putting down a revolt in north Germany. Now the German bishops who supported the Emperor declared that Gregory was deposed: this caused some of Henry IV's subjects in south Germany to rebel, and insist on him being reconciled with the Pope by 1077. The Pope was actually journeying north to support the rebels when he paused to rest at Canossa castle. Faced by the penitent Emperor he had no

The conflict between Henry IV and Gregory VII as shown by a German chronicler about a hundred years after the event. On the left the Emperor is seated with a rival Pope appointed by himself; on the right Gregory is driven from Rome; at the bottom he dies in exile at Salerno

Harvest time in the Middle Ages, from a late twelfth century German manuscript

choice but to lift the excommunication and take him back into the
Church.

But this reconciliation was only
a lull in the contest between
Henry and Gregory, and their
successors as Emperor and Pope.
Henry's position as king within
Germany was weakened, but
Gregory's fate was worse. The
appalling conduct in Rome of the
Pope's new allies, the Normans,
made it impossible for him to stay
in the city, and he died exiled in
southern Italy in 1085.

The question of lay appointment
was temporarily settled in 1122
when Pope and Emperor agreed
to a form of appointment which
gave them both a share in the
ceremonies. But the argument
about the rights of Pope and
Emperor to intervene in the affairs
of State and Church respectively
rumbled on throughout the
Middle Ages.

THE WEALTH OF CHURCH AND STATE

1   Farming

During the Middle Ages most
wealth came from the land, which
was divided between lay landlords and the Church in the form
of huge estates. In both cases the
actual farming was done by the
peasants. Few of them owned any
land, and they were prevented
from leaving the service of their
local landlord by custom and law.
They were made to work on their
lord's fields and pay certain taxes
(D6,7). The landlord employed a
steward to supervise them.

Farming methods were very
inefficient by comparison with
today. The most important piece
of equipment was the plough,
which changed little over the
centuries. It was usually drawn
by four oxen. Because the oxen
could not turn easily the furrows
were long and straight. This
resulted in large open fields.

Famine and illness were never
far away. The Black Death, which
wiped out about a third of the
population of Europe between
1345 and 1380, was only the
worst epidemic of a disease which
persisted throughout the Middle
Ages (D8). Peasant life was a
continual struggle against death,
starvation and the seasons of the
year, which demanded a heavy
and fixed round of tasks to be
done at the correct time if food
was to be grown and harvested
(D9).

After 1100 a generally increasing population brought a greater
demand for food. Some peasants
became more prosperous and paid
their lords a rent instead of
labouring for them. In France
many new farms were founded in
the country round Paris in which
the tenants were able to escape
from being tied to one lord by
law (D10). In Poland and further
east enterprising men set themselves up as free farmers on old
Slav lands.

A leading part in the expansion
of settlement and farming between
1100 and 1300 was played by the
Church and especially by the
Cistercian order of monks. The
Cistercians developed their estates
into large profitable farms, and in
England they became famous for

The counting house of an Italian banker in the fifteenth century

Flemish dyers at work in Belgium in 1492

A crusading knight fighting the Muslims

their sheep runs worked by men who were attached to the monastery. Their wool became the most important of England's exports in the Middle Ages.

2   Towns and Trade

The increase of population in the later Middle Ages led to an expansion of trade and to the growth of towns. Trade routes linked the various regions of Europe and brought Europe into closer contact with Asia. Trade could bring high profits. Bankers and money lenders often did well out of interest rates which could be as high as thirty or forty per cent, although money lending was frowned upon by the Church. Gradually these developments began to lessen the importance of land as a source of wealth, a situation which laymen were more able to exploit than the Church.

Annual fairs were events of great importance. Here the merchants met and exchanged goods and, particularly in the towns of north Italy, developed new business and trading practices. These included bills of exchange, and shared capital enterprises, all of which helped them to make their business more secure and efficient, and to build up great fortunes.

In the towns the richer merchants and the craftsmen in a particular craft came together to form guilds which regulated the entry to that occupation and fixed the prices of goods and commodities. The guildsmen were granted privileges and rights which before had belonged to landlords (D11). In the same way towns joined together to form trading organizations which gave privileges and 'protection' to individual merchants (D12). The most famous of these was the Hanseatic League in north Germany.

The greatest and most prosperous towns of the Middle Ages were in Germany, Holland and Italy. By the fourteenth century they had reached the size of an average English town today, with populations of about 100,000 (D13). The wool manufacturing and wool finishing industries brought immense wealth to a number of great families who spent their money beautifying their cities with impressive public buildings.

Although guilds and town councils eventually became closed groups concerned only with preserving their own privileges, at the time of their growth they produced new ideas which questioned the traditional values of medieval society. It was in the north Italian towns that the Holy Roman Emperor's claim to rule was first challenged. A number of the towns later set up their own local governments. It was in the German towns at the end of the Middle Ages that the views of Martin Luther and other Protestant reformers found most support. *(Luther, Erasmus and Loyola)**

By this time the merchant had become a person whose wealth and position was greatly envied (D14).

3   Industry

Although the society of medieval Europe was mainly rural, there was a certain amount of industry. Wine making and brewing were important on a small scale in the home or on the estate, but between 1100 and 1300 sheep farming developed into an international industry. The raw wool was exported from England to Belgium and Italy to be made into cloth. Usually the English peasant farmer only took on weaving in addition to his traditional work, and even successful wool merchants often grew crops on their land. In Belgium and Italy, however, men became specialists in the finishing – dying, napping and cutting – of

*Titles in brackets refer to other booklets in the Program

Pope Innocent III, who skilfully exploited the weakness of the Empire after the death of Henry IV to establish the lay power of the papacy

cloth, so more industrialized methods became common. Dying vats, weaving looms and drying frames were assembled in factories and men worked them for wages. The cost of providing the equipment was so high that the richer craftsmen bought out the poorer ones, and came to control the workers they employed.

Other important industries were mining, especially in Germany and Poland, and shipbuilding, in the seafaring countries of Europe.

THE CRUSADES 1096-1204

During the two centuries after Canossa the authority of the Church increased throughout Europe. Its power was most dramatically shown by a movement begun by Pope Urban II in 1096 known as the Crusades. These were wars of conquest led by the Church to win back the Holy Land of Palestine, where Jesus Christ had lived and taught. Along with many other former parts of the Byzantine Empire it was then in the hands of the Muslims. *(Constantine)*

The Pope's appeal to Church and State to take up arms in the cause of Christianity met with a remarkable response. The Crusades were supported by all classes of society from kings and nobles down to peasants and children. The Italian trading cities contributed money and later transport. Despite their ignorance of local conditions and their lack of proper military organization, the Crusaders showed enough bravery and determination to capture Jerusalem in 1099. They established a colony to defend their conquests, and built a series of massive castles to protect the coastal strip of the eastern Mediterranean from the Muslims in the Syrian desert.

There is no doubt that for

many the Crusades, and especially the First, were an expression of genuine religious feeling: the Church regarded the Crusaders as pilgrims. But as time went on their motives generally became more worldly and less idealistic. The Venetians provided a fleet for the Fourth Crusade purely because they hoped to turn the campaign to their own commercial advantage, which they succeeded in doing. Greed for land and trading privileges became increasingly dominant, and in the thirteenth century the idea of a Crusade was used by Popes to justify acts of war against their political enemies, Christian or not.

Although the Muslims eventually regained control over the Holy Land, there were advantages for western Europe from the Crusades. Trade between Muslims and Crusaders enabled the luxury goods of the East to reach Europe. The nobles of both sides had a certain amount of personal contact with each other which resulted in an exchange of ideas, although they never accepted that there was much truth in each other's religions. The Crusades showed how all classes of society could unite to face a challenge, and how the ideal of partnership between Church and State could work in practice. Finally, they showed the strength of belief in Christianity at that time by the fact that men were willing to give up to it their money and often their lives.

THE POPE AND THE EMPEROR AFTER CANOSSA

Gregory VII's ideas of papal monarchy were most strongly enforced in the reign of Pope Innocent III (1198-1216). He excommunicated King John of England and took the offensive against non-Christians and heretics (usually those with unconventional Christian beliefs). He compared his power over the Holy Roman Emperor to that of the sun over the moon.

The position of the Holy Roman Emperor in Europe became weaker. Although the Emperor Frederick I (called Barbarossa) did temporarily succeed in breaking the power of the nobles in Germany in the later part of the twelfth century, his son Frederick II could not restore the Imperial Government which had broken down during his father's struggles with the nobles. When Frederick II died while marching to fight the Pope in 1250 he was, like Henry IV before him, excommunicated. With his death the medieval Empire came to an end. As the princes in Germany strengthened their position, the Imperial and royal titles came to be of little importance compared with the privileges of the seven princes who elected the Emperor (D17).

FRANCE

In France, however, the king became stronger whilst the Church and nobles grew weaker. This was especially so in the reign of Philip Augustus (1180-1227) who extended the royal lands from a small area round Paris to include almost the whole of present-day France. He gave peasants rights in the land at the expense of the

The papal palace at Avignon as it appeared in the seventeenth century

feudal lords. He granted many charters to new towns and so made an ally of the townspeople, whose services he was then able to use for the taxation and skills which his new system of government required. Later, in the reign of Philip IV, the Church became extremely unpopular in France because Pope Boniface VIII forbade the payment of taxes to the State and insisted on the superiority of Church and Pope over State and king.

ENGLAND

Here the crown also became increasingly dependent on merchants, lawyers and woolmen, so that by the reign of Edward III (1327-77) the wars with Scotland and France were largely financed by taxes and loans from merchants. Anti-Church feeling had grown so strong that Parliament passed laws which restricted the Church's legal powers in England.

Gradually a new view of society began to develop. Some writers argued that the State and its ruler should be completely independent of the authority of the Church. They also argued that the wealth and power of the Church were too great: the Church should have spiritual and moral influence but not political power.

THE CHURCH AT THE END OF THE MIDDLE AGES

For half a century after 1309 the Popes were forced to live at Avignon, papal territory in southern France, and not in Rome. This was the result of disorder in Italy, and of a series of quarrels between the Popes and various European kings. On its return to Rome in 1378 the papacy was too weak even to decide who was to become

The Bishop of Chartres in his cathedral school. Chartres, in France, was a centre for the teaching of astronomy and logic before the rise of the University of Paris

the next Pope, let alone attempt to control the political affairs of Europe.

Eventually a series of internal reforms were carried out, and general councils of the Church met to discuss the Church's teaching and organization. These councils accepted that ordinary lay people should play a greater part in the life of the Church, instead of simply submitting themselves unquestioningly to its authority.

This idea was later taken up by Martin Luther and other protestant reformers of the sixteenth century, but they went much further and denied the authority of the Pope. (*Luther, Erasmus and Loyola*) The widespread feeling that the Church needed to be reformed led, in those countries which followed the protestant reformers, to the seizure of Church property by the State and to a thorough change in religious beliefs.

EDUCATION: SCHOOLS AND UNIVERSITIES

The intellectual life of Europe changed too. In the early Middle Ages all learning was undertaken in cathedral and monastic schools where clerks were taught to read and write. The clerks also needed enough understanding of mathematics to be able to work out the feast days of the Christian year and enough musical knowledge to conduct the Church services. All study was carried out by churchmen and the only books used were the Bible and the works of the early Christian writers. It is not surprising that the authority of the Pope and the tradition and law of the Church were not seriously questioned.

The age of the Crusades, with its growth of trade and towns, saw the development of cathedral schools into universities, first at Bologna, then Paris, Salerno and Oxford and, by the fourteenth century, throughout Europe. Studies widened to take in medicine and law in addition to the traditional arts and theology. Contact with the Muslim and Byzantine Empires renewed interest in and knowledge of Greek philosophy and science.

The teaching of the Church was re-examined (D18). Although the greatest medieval scholar, St Thomas Aquinas, believed that reason and Christianity were not opposed to each other, there was no general agreement on the problem and it was the subject of increasing argument in the later Middle Ages. (*The Scientific Revolution*)

The universities were sited in towns, and their charters were usually given by kings and princes. The Church was never able to dominate the universities as it had the monastic and cathedral schools. Young men from the universities were very much in demand at the courts of Europe because of their training in the art of government. Although logic, philosophy and theology remained the main studies until the end of the Middle Ages, in the fifteenth century private academies revived the study of Greek and Roman history and literature. As the *Renaissance* (*Leonardo da Vinci*) spread throughout Europe, this new non-Church curriculum came to dominate the schools and universities, and learning passed outside the Church's control (D20).

MEDIEVAL EUROPE AND WORLD HISTORY

Throughout the world societies have governments and religious systems, but only in medieval Europe did they come into such long conflict with each other. The explanation must belong to western Europe alone. Medieval Europe grew out of the collapse of the Roman Empire *(Constantine)*: the Church took over some of its functions and the emperors, kings and barons took over others. In an attempt to sort out the confusion Europeans created the idea of the two chains of authority — lay and holy. But the idea had little to do with the real world and inevitably led to conflict.

In the end the medieval European system collapsed because of changes inside Europe. With the rise of trade and industry, land ceased to be the only large source of wealth; the feudal system was weakened; and separate kingdoms became more powerful at the expense of emperor and nobles. Although the universal Church could defeat the Emperor it was no match for the new kingdoms. The rise of the universities caused

The Donation of Constantine. A thirteenth century wall-painting showing the Emperor Constantine giving both spiritual and lay power throughout the Roman Empire to Pope Sylvester. Although the event never took place, it provided the basis for the Pope's claims to political power

a decline in the educational and cultural role of the Church. In particular the monasteries lost much of their importance. Europe was moving towards a new system marked by the Renaissance and the Reformation. (*Leonardo da Vinci; Luther, Erasmus and Loyola*)

DOCUMENT 1

CANOSSA   *POPE GREGORY VII – His description of the penance of Henry IV at Canossa, 1077*

He [Henry] also, before entering Italy, sent on to us suppliant legates, offering in all things to render satisfaction to God, to St Peter and to us. And he renewed his promise that, besides amending his life, he would observe all obedience if only he might merit to obtain from us the favour of absolution and the apostolic benediction. When, after long deferring this and holding frequent consultations, we had, through all the envoys who passed, severely taken him [Henry] to task for his excesses: he came at length of his own accord, with a few followers, showing nothing of hostility or boldness, to the town of Canossa where we were tarrying. And there, having laid aside all the belongings of royalty, wretchedly, with bare feet and clad in wool, he continued for three days to stand before the gate of the castle. Nor did he desist from imploring with many tears the aid and consolation of the apostolic mercy until he had moved all of those who were present there.

DOCUMENT 2

APPOINTING BISHOPS   *CARDINAL HUMBERT – His attack on the practice of appointment by those outside the Church*

The supreme bishops who must be venerated throughout the world have decreed at the dictation of the Holy Spirit that [in episcopal elections] the choice made by the clergy shall be confirmed by the decision of the metropolitan [archbishop], and the request of laity and people by the consent of the prince. But everything is in fact done in a perverted order, in rejection of the holy canons and in utter contempt of the whole Christian religion, and the first things come last and the last first. For the lay authority comes first in electing and confirming and then, willy-nilly, the consent of laity, people and clergy follows, and the metropolitan's decision comes last of all. Men preferred by this means are not to be numbered among the bishops, because what ought to be done to them last is in fact done first, and done by men who have no business with it.

DOCUMENT 3

THE WEALTH OF THE CHURCH   *Land is given to the Abbey of Winchcombe. From a document of about 1180*

Know all men, present and future, that I Robert, clerk of Alne, have . . . given to the said monks for ever, to the health of mine own soul and of that of Alice my wife and our ancestors, all my land at Alne between the two valleys, called Kendresled. In return for which donation the monks have granted me twenty shillings, and a monk's allowance of bread and beer such as are daily laid on the refectory table, so often as I may come to Winchcombe on their business or mine own. Moreover, they have granted to receive me at my latter end as a monk; and to Alice my wife they have granted her part in all good deeds which are done or shall be done in the convent of Winchcombe, and burial at her latter end if she desire it.

DOCUMENT 4

THE POWER OF THE POPE   *Jottings from Pope Gregory's notebook*

1 That only the Bishop of Rome is by law called universal
2 That he alone may depose or reinstate bishops
3 That his legate may preside over all the bishops in council, even should he be inferior in rank, and may pronounce sentence of deposition against them
4 That the Pope may depose persons in their absence
5 That, among other things, he must not stay under the same roof with persons whom he has excommunicated
6 That the Pope is the only man whose feet shall be kissed by all princes
7 That his title alone shall be read out in churches
8 That his title is unique in all the world
9 That he may depose Emperors
10 That he must not be judged by anyone
11 That no one shall dare to condemn one who appeals to the Apostolic See
12 That the Pope can absolve the subjects of the wicked from their fealty to them

DOCUMENT 5

THE EXCOMMUNICATION OF HENRY IV *GREGORY VII –*
A letter to the German clergy

I forbid King Henry, son of the Emperor Henry, who has rebelled with
unheard-of insolence against your Church, to govern any part of the
Kingdom of the Germans or of Italy; and I absolve all Christians from
any oaths to him which they have already taken or shall take in the
future, and I forbid anyone to serve him as if he were King. For it is
right that one who seeks to detract from the honour of your Church
shall himself lose the honour which is accorded him. And because he has
refused to obey as a Christian and has not returned to God, whom he
has deserted by associating with excommunicated men, by spurning the
warning which (as you are my witness) I issued for his own salvation,
and by withdrawing from your Church in an attempt to sunder it
apart: in your place I bind him with the chain of anathema
[excommunication].

DOCUMENT 6

THE STEWARD'S DUTIES *Instructions to the steward of a royal
estate in France in the early Middle Ages*

Whenever our stewards are to see that our work is performed – sowing,
ploughing, harvesting, cutting of hay, or gathering of grapes – let each
of them at the proper time and place supervise and give directions how
the work is to be done, so that it may be done well . . . .
   We wish that our stewards pay a full tenth of all produce to the
churches which are on our property . . . .
   Every steward should perform his full service as he has been
directed. And if necessity requires that he should serve additional time,
he should determine whether he should increase the [day] service or the
night service.
   The stewards should keep in the barns of our principal estates no
fewer than a hundred chickens and thirty geese; or on smaller farms let
them have no fewer than fifty chickens and twelve geese.
   Every steward should always send the produce [of the chickens and
geese] to our court abundantly throughout the year, except when they
make visits three or four or more times.
   Every steward should keep fish ponds on our estates where they were
in the past. He should enlarge them if possible . . . .

DOCUMENT 7

DEATH DUES   *The rights of a French abbot in 1291*

My lord abbot of St Ouen takes to his own share all the movable goods of each of his tenants in the parish of Quincampoist when they die, and all that may come or belong to the said dead man by law, except that he shall leave all these utensils here following, to wit, the bastard cart and the plough and the [barrow] and [sheaf-cart] and the [cider-crusher] and the mortar and pestle and the winnowing-fan and the bushel-measure and the kneading trough and one sack for grinding his corn, and a sieve for his meal and a basket and the worst chest in his house for a bedstead, and a spade and an axe, a fork for pitching sheaves and a dung-fork, a gridiron and a trivet, and one bed, if there be more than one, and a brass pot if the aforesaid utensils are in his house; and all other movables go to my lord abbot.

DOCUMENT 8

THE BLACK DEATH   *The insecurity of life in the Middle Ages – an Italian writer describes the Black Death in Florence in 1348*

Not only conversation and contact with the sick carried the illness to the healthy and was cause of their common death. Even the clothing or other things touched or used by the sick seem to carry with them that same disease . . . . If an animal outside the human species contacted the belongings of a man sick or dead of this illness, it not only caught the disease, but within a brief time was killed by it. My own eyes . . . saw one day (and other times besides) this occurrence. The rags of a poor man dead from this disease had been thrown in a public street. Two pigs came to them with their snouts, and then seized them with their teeth and tossed them about with their jaws. A short hour later, after some staggering as if the poison was taking effect, both of them fell dead to earth upon the rags which they had unhappily dragged.

DOCUMENT 9

THE MISERABLE PLIGHT OF THE PEASANTS   *A German priest writing in 1520*

. . . Their condition is very wretched and hard. They live apart from the rest in lowly fashion, each with his own household and his beasts. Their cottages are of mud and timber, rising little above the ground, and covered with straw. They feed on brown bread, oatmeal, porridge, or boiled peas; they drink water or whey. They are clad in a linen coat, with boots of untanned leather and a dyed cap. They are ever an unquiet crew, laborious and unclean. They bring to the nearest town whatsoever each hath gained either from his field or from the produce of his flocks; and here they buy in return whatsoever each needeth; for they have few or no artificers dwelling among them. On holy days, they come all together in the morning to the church, whereof there is commonly one for each village; there they hear from their priest God's word and the sacraments; then after noon they treat of their own affairs under a linden tree or in some other public place. After this, the younger folk dance to the sound of the pipe, while the elders go to the tavern and drink wine. None goeth unarmed in public; each hath his sword by his side for any chance emergency . . . . The peasants have to work often-times in the year for their lord, tilling the fields, sowing and reaping and gathering into the barns, carrying wood, building, and digging ditches. There is nothing which this servile and wretched folk is not said to owe to these [lords] ; nor is there anything which, if the lord bid them do it, they dare to refuse without peril; the defaulter is heavily punished. Yet there is nothing which they feel more hardly than this, than the greater part of the fields which they occupy are not their own.

DOCUMENT 10

A FREE TENANT   *From the king's charter to the French town of Lorris, given in 1155*

Whoever has his farm in the parish of Lorris shall lose none of it by fines, unless he has been fined for an offence against us or any of our new settlers.

No one going to or coming from the fairs or the market of Lorris shall be arrested or disturbed, unless he committed an offence on that same day.

No man need leave Lorris in order to plead in the court of the king.

No man of Lorris should labour for us except once a year, to bring our wine to Orleans. Nor are others to do this, but only those who have horses and wagons and have been summoned. They shall not receive lodging from us. The villeins shall bring wood for our kitchen.

Whoever lives in the parish of Lorris one year and a day with no demand having been made for him, if he was not denied the right by us or by our [sheriff], from that time he shall remain free and undisturbed.

DOCUMENT 11

THE PRIVILEGES OF GUILDS   *Privileges granted by the Bishop of*
Worms to the Guild of Fishermen in the town

In the name of the Holy and Undivided Trinity. Be it known . . . that
Adalbert, the venerable Bishop of Worms, has appointed these twenty-
three fishermen of Worms namely these [named] . . . . To them he
gives this privilege under this condition: that if any of them should
succumb to death, his nearest relative may succeed him in this office by
hereditary custom; if however there is no heir, the place should be filled
to the above number by the common counsel of the city [fishermen].
On the advice of the above-mentioned men, the bishop has also decreed
that if anyone should be found buying fish between Suelntheim and
Altdruphen for the sake of reselling them, and should be caught in this
purchase, the fish should be taken from him and divided equally among
the city [fishermen].

DOCUMENT 12

A FEDERATION OF TOWNS   *The declaration of a group of*
Westphalian towns

We hereby make known to all men, now and in the future, that
because of the manifold dangers to which we are constantly exposed,
of capture, robbery, and many other injuries, we have . . . decided to
unite in a perpetual confederation under the following terms and we
have mutually given and received word and oath: first, that if any
man shall take captive one of our citizens or seize his goods without just
cause, we will altogether deny to him opportunity to trade in all our
cities aforesaid. And if the [steward] of any lord shall be the author of
an injury that has been done, the aforementioned privileges shall be
altogether witheld from the lord of that steward and from all his
soldiers and servants, and all others dwelling with him in his castle . . . .
If any robber has taken goods from one of our citizens . . . and the
injured man shall go to any one of our [federated] cities seeking counsel
and aid, in order that justice may be done upon the malefactor, the
citizens of that city shall act as they would be obliged to act if executing
justice for a similar crime committed against one of their own fellow
citizens.

DOCUMENT 13

FLORENCE   *A description of the city in 1338*

It has been estimated that there are in Florence upwards of 90,000 mouths, including men, women and children, from the evidence of the bread which is continuously needed in the city . . . . It has been guessed that there were continuously in the city more than 1,500 foreigners, transients and soldiers, not counting in the total . . . friars and cloistered nuns . . . . It has been estimated that there were in these times in the countryside and district of Florence upwards of 80,000 men . . . . We have discovered that the boys and girls who are learning to read number 8,000 to 10,000. The boys who are learning the abacus and calculation in six schools number from 1100 to 1200. And those who are learning Latin and logic in four large schools number from 550 to 600.

The shops of the wool craft were 200 or more, and produced from 70,000 to 80,000 cloths, which were worth upwards of 1,200,000 gold florins. A third of this value remained in the country to pay for labour, without regarding the profit which the wool merchants made from that labour. More than 30,000 persons were supported by it.

DOCUMENT 14

THE IMPORTANCE OF MERCHANTS   *A merchant of Naples at the close of the Middle Ages gives his view of the importance of his profession*

The dignity and office of merchants is great and exalted in many respects. They bring about an abundance of money, jewels, gold, silver, and all kinds of metals. They bring about an abundance of guilds of various crafts. Hence, cities and countries are driven to cultivate the land, to enlarge the herds, and to exploit the incomes and rents. And [merchants] through their activity enable the poor to live; through their initiative in tax farming they promote the activity of administration; through their exports and imports of merchandise they cause the customs and excises of the lords and republics to expand, and consequently they enlarge the public and common treasury.

DOCUMENT 15

THE FIRST CRUSADE   *POPE URBAN II – His call for a Crusade given at Clermont in 1095*

O children of God, since you have promised God, more earnestly than usual, to keep the peace among yourselves and faithfully preserve and maintain the rights of the Church, it is vital that you should make a rapid expedition to help your brothers who live in the east, who need your assistance and have now many times appealed for it. For, as most of you have already been told, they have been invaded as far as the Mediterranean sea, up to the point called the arm of St George, by the Turks, a Persian people, who have overrun an increasing amount of Christian territory on the frontiers of Romania, and have conquered and overcome your brothers seven times over in war . . . .

DOCUMENT 16

TRADE   *A Muslim traveller describes trading relations between Crusaders and Muslims*

The Christians impose a tax on the Muslims in their land which gives them full security; and likewise the Christian merchants pay a tax upon their goods in Muslim lands. Agreement exists between them, and there is equal treatment in all cases. The soldiers engage themselves in their war while the people are at peace and the world goes to him who conquers.

DOCUMENT 17

CHOOSING THE HOLY ROMAN EMPEROR   *These rules, laid down in 1356, show the importance of the princes who elected the Emperor*

We decree and determine by this Imperial edict that whenever the electoral princes are summoned according to the ancient and praise-worthy custom to meet and elect a king of the Romans and future Emperor, each one of them shall be bound to furnish on demand an escort and safe conduct to his fellow electors or their representatives . . . .

We decree and command also that all other princes who hold fiefs from the Empire by whatever title . . . shall furnish escort and safe conduct for this occasion to every electoral prince or his representatives, on demand, within their own lands and as much further as they can . . . .

It shall be the duty of the Archbishop of Mainz to send notice of the approaching election to each of the electoral princes by his messenger . . . .

When news of the death of the king of the Romans has been received at Mainz, within one month from the date of receiving it the Archbishop of Mainz shall send notices of the death and of the approaching elections to all the electoral princes . . . .

DOCUMENT 18

AN INQUIRING APPROACH TO STUDY   *PETER ABELARD —*
The medieval scholar writing in 1122

In view of these considerations, I have ventured to bring together various
dicta [sayings] of the holy fathers, as they came to mind, and to formu-
late certain questions which were suggested by the seeming contradictions
in the statements. These questions ought to serve to excite tender
readers to a zealous inquiry into truth and so sharpen their wits. The
master key of knowledge is, indeed, a persistent and frequent questioning.
Aristotle, the most clear-sighted of all the philosophers, was desirous
above all things else to arouse this questioning spirit . . . . By doubting we
come to examine, and by examining we reach the truth.

DOCUMENT 19

STUDENT PRIVILEGES   *PHILIP AUGUSTUS — The king of*
France grants privileges to the students of the University of Paris
in 1200

. . . Neither our [sheriff] nor our judges shall lay hands on a student for
any offence whatever; nor shall they place him in our prison, unless such
a crime has been committed by the student, that he ought to be
arrested. And in that case, our judge shall arrest him on the spot,
without striking him at all, unless he resists, and shall hand him over
to the ecclesiastical judge, who ought to guard him in order to satisfy
us and the one suffering the injury. And if a serious crime has been
committed, our judge shall go or shall send to see what is done with
the student.

DOCUMENT 20

STUDENT LIFE   *A thirteenth century writer describes the conduct*
of students at the University of Paris

They affirmed that the English were drunkards and had tails; the sons of
France proud, effeminate and carefully adorned like women. They said
that the Germans were furious and obscene at their feasts; the Normans,
vain and boastful; the Poitevans, traitors and always adventurers. The
Burgundians they considered vulgar and stupid. The Bretons were reputed
to be fickle and changeable . . . . The Lombards were called avaricious,
vicious and cowardly; the Romans, seditious, turbulent and slanderous;
the Sicilians, tyrannical and cruel; the inhabitants of Brabant, men of
blood, incendiaries, brigands and ravishers; the Flemish, fickle, prodigal,
gluttonous, yielding as butter, and slothful. After such insults from
words they often came to blows.

ACKNOWLEDGMENTS

Illustrations

Bibliothèque Nationale, Paris page 3 top; Staatsbibliothek, Munich page 3 bottom; Scala page 4; Trustees of the British Museum pages 7, 14; Professor K.J. Conant page 8; Master and Fellows of Corpus Christi College, Cambridge page 9; Universitätbibliothek, Jena page 11; Reinisches Landesmuseum, Bonn page 12; Archivo di Stato, Siena page 13; Musée des Monuments Français, Paris page 15; Musée Calvet, Avignon page 19; The Mansell Collection page 22.

Documents

D2, 4, 5, 15, *Sources for the History of Medieval Europe,* Bryan Pullan, Basil Blackwell; D6, 8, 10, 11, 13, 18, 19 *Medieval Culture and Society,* D. Herlihy, Harper & Row; D14, *Medieval Trade in the Mediterranean World,* R.S. Lopez and I.W. Raymond, Columbia University Press; D16, *A History of Medieval Europe,* R.H.C. Davis, Longman; *Translations and Reprints of the Original Sources of European History, Vol. II,* University of Pennsylvania Press.